THE
CHARGE
OF THE GODDESS

THE POETRY OF
DOREEN VALIENTE

EXPANDED EDITION

Published by The Doreen Valiente Foundation
in association with The Centre For Pagan Studies

Design & Layout: Ashley Mortimer / The Doreen Valiente Foundation

Editing & Transcription: Ashley Mortimer & Caz Galloway

Technical Consultant: Rick Falconer

Cover Painting: Marc Potts

Printed by Lightning Source International

Published by The Doreen Valiente Foundation
in association with The Centre For Pagan Studies

First printing 2014

ISBN   978-0-9928430-0-7

EAN

www.doreenvaliente.org
www.centre-for-pagan-studies.com

FOREWORD

Doreen Valiente was one of the most remarkable people that my wife Julie and I have ever met and we both feel absolutely privileged to have called her our friend as well as my working magical partner and the patron of The Centre For Pagan Studies. We cared for Doreen when she became ill at the end of her life and just before she died I asked her if there was anything that she had really wanted to do but hadn't. I was surprised to hear that there was an enormous amount of her poetry that had not been published. She had once been invited to speak at the Poetry Society but apparently they had turned her down for membership because she was a witch! She explained that she wanted to put her poems in a book but her publishers were not keen on becoming known as a poetry publishers. They had told her that if they had been, Doreen's book would have been at the top of their list. I saw that this was something she greatly regretted and I made her a promise to publish such a book so the world could enjoy her poetry and know just how talented she was.

Doreen bequeathed to me her very famous and extensive collection of Witchcraft and Folklore items, plus her 2,000-volume library and all her copyrights. I wanted to know what she thought I should do with all of this but all she told me rather enigmatically was that she was sure that I would "do the right thing". Eventually I realised what she had meant by this and so, in 2011, The Doreen Valiente Foundation was established as a charitable trust and I handed the ownership of Doreen's entire legacy to the Foundation so that it can now never be sold, given away or split up and will be preserved forever as publicly owned heritage for all time.

With the advent of the Foundation things have moved on considerably. The CFPS has grown and worked with the DVF to continue to utilize Doreen's legacy to educate the wider public about folklore traditions and we have organized many events in persuit of this charitable aim. In 2013 we achieved something remarkable by getting a Heritage Blue Plaque placed upon the council block of flats where Doreen lived for over 30 years making her the first Witch to be honoured in this way. We are currently working on further Blue Plaques and other events to honour the likes of Gerald Gardner, Patricia Crowther and others who were friends and colleagues of Doreen.

A year after Doreen died I had approached two friends who ran the Hexagon Archive about the idea of a poetry book. They went straight to work and published the first version of this book; now sold out. The book was not, however, a complete picture of her work, it served as a taster of what was to come regarding the poems, collection and legacy. I also rather hated the photograph that I was staged to sit because it made me look like a medieval warlord!

With all the hard lessons we have learned and the new skills we have developed while working with CFPS and DVF we are now, finally, able to properly make good my promise to Doreen by publishing her poems under our own publishing arm with help from some skilled and trusted friends, and I think Doreen would be as delighted as I am to be able to say that every penny earned as a result of you buying this book will go directly into the Foundation funds so that Doreen's legacy and that of others who have donated their precious artefacts to the Doreen Valiente Collection can be researched, restored, preserved and enjoyed ... by all of us ... for all time.

John Belham-Payne
Doreen Valiente Foundation
The Centre For Pagan Studies

MEMORIES OF DOREEN

Jean Williams: I first met Doreen about fifteen years ago, at a Grand Sabbat in a wood in Surrey. She cast the circle with her broomstick, taking command of the space. She then appeared to grow to immense stature as, broomstick in hand, she summoned the Mighty Ones to guard the circle. I have never before, or since, witnessed such natural authority.

Marian Green: Doreen believed in the magic of the heart and could charm the birds from the trees. Her legacy to modern Witchcraft is often overlooked, yet The Charge, recited by Wiccans everywhere, came from her inspiration, and much of the ritual found in books was her work. I hope more people have the opportunity of experiencing her writing for many years to come.

Ralph Harvey: When future generations look back on the 20th Century and the resurgence of "The Old Religion", Doreen Valiente's name will dominate. Modest and retiring, she never sought the publicity that has so regretfully marred the Craft with the antics of some self-professed Witches. The world in general and particularly the world of Witchcraft has been enriched by her presence on Earth, and Doreen's passing into her beloved Summerlands has left us all the poorer. Our loss is the Old Gods' gain.

Lois Bourne: Doreen was loquacious and disarming, but behind her pleasant personality was a steely determination not to suffer fools gladly. She had the remarkable ability to discern quite quickly the difference between truth and fiction, but no one in genuine trouble or misfortune was ever turned away. She was a true friend, faithful and loyal to her calling.

Janet Farrar: "Hob" was a coconut man. Doreen had found him on one of her sorties around the antique shops of Brighton. He may well have started life in the Caribbean and travelled with a sailor back to England. He was "alive" when Doreen found him and she made him her house guardian, sometimes her grin and Hob's seemed to match the other. When Doreen passed into the Summerlands, my heart went out to that funny little coconut familiar. How lonely he must have felt, afraid of what was to become of him. At least now he knows that he is loved and considered useful. I am sure that next time we meet we will both have a wink in our eye for each other. So here's looking at you, Hob old friend. There are good times yet to be had for coconuts and familiars alike!

Patricia Crowther: Memories of my friend Doreen Valiente are deep and abiding and still fresh in my mind since the day we met nearly forty years ago. I greatly valued Doreen's friendship and there was always excitement, discovery, laughter and the sharing of sacred rites with this fascinating lady.

Poetry reveals the beauty of the soul and these pages certainly substantiate the truth of this opinion. My feelings concerning Doreen are perfectly expressed in the following lines by Robert Louis Stevenson:

> Honour, anger, valour, fire,
> A love that life could never tire;
> Death quench or evil stir,
> The Mighty Maker gave to her

The Origins Of "The Charge Of The Goddess"

The reason for believing that Doreen Valiente wrote the Charge Of The Goddess is simply that all the available evidence suggests that she did! Gerald Gardner's books of rites show the Charge developing in the 1940s and early 1950s from a pastiche of Crowley's writing to one of Charles Godfrey Leland and Crowley. What Doreen did was to keep the Leland, which she thought more authentic, put in a new framework, and write the "White Moon Charge", which is wholly original in its words, although its basic form, of a universal nature goddess identified with the moon and addressing her devotees, is based on Apuleius's "Metamorphoses", from ancient Rome. Nothing like Doreen's words for the White Moon Charge have been found in any older text, and they gave Wicca a theology as well as its finest piece of liturgy. I think that Doreen's way of composing was to take an idea, a word or even a single phrase (never more) from an older text and then to create a completely new piece of work underneath it. So it was with her half of the Charge.

Professor Ronald Hutton

EDITORS' PREFACE

When we sat down to compile this book we were under the impression it was going to be a fairly straightforward re-print of the previous edition of "Charge Of The Goddess" with a few extra poems. As we began to transcribe the text and add the poetry we found in Doreen's collection of manuscripts and documents, mostly unpublished, we began to realise that the project had grown almost logarithmically and evolved from "collection" almost to "anthology".

Lacking Doreen's insight, we debated endlessly the best way of structuring the book to best present the poems and stories until, finally, it came to us, the oldest observed structure we know: the seasons. Each season has universal themes, the correspondences and emotions we experienced as we reviewed the material with a combination of common sense, specialist knowledge and intuitive instinct helped us to divide them up with almost unanimous agreement. In Spring we found the poetry that dwells on youth, growth, innocence and, perhaps, naivety. The Summer poems evoked a sense of mischief, adventure, sexuality and the beginnings of responsibility while Autumn showed the juxtaposition of Doreen's deep maturity and wry humour before, finally, Winter combined themes of death, parting and stillness with the hope for new life and new beginnings in the deep mysteries of rebirth and reincarnation. We find ourselves hoping that the reader will permit mood and inspiration to indicate which season holds sudden interest, answers or solace and we have a pleasingly intuitive inkling that we may have succeeded in presenting Doreen's work as she would have wished.

We're deeply indebted to the people who contributed advice and material who, together with those who contributed their time, dedication, affection and great spirit and energy have made our role as editors and publishers into a pleasure beyond expectation. What we hope we've achieved is to fulfil some of the deeper aims of the Doreen Valiente Foundation: to bring people together to share and celebrate the incredible legacy she left as we now invite an increasingly wider audience to do just this as the readers of these poems, without whom any list of thanks and acknowledgements would be as pointless as it would be incomplete.

Ashley Mortimer
Caz Galloway

EDITORS' ACKNOWLEDGEMENTS

The editors would like to personally thank the following for their support and contributions to the publication of this edition of The Charge Of The Goddess:

John Belham-Payne, Julie Belham-Payne, Professor Ronald Hutton, Patricia Crowther, Jean Williams, Marian Green, Ralph Harvey, Lois Bourne, Janet Farrar, Marc Potts, Rick Falconer, Sarah Kay, Philip Heselton, The members and honorary members of The Doreen Valiente Foundation.

CONTENTS

The Charge Of The Goddess

SPRING

SUMMER

AUTUMN

WINTER

The Witch's Chant

THE
CHARGE
OF THE GODDESS

THE CHARGE OF THE GODDESS

Listen to the words of the Great Mother, who was of old also called Artemis; Astarte; Diana; Melusine; Aphrodite; Cerridwen; Dana; Arianrhod; Isis; Bride; and by many other names.

Whenever ye have need of anything, once in a month, and better it be when the Moon be full, then ye shall assemble in some secret place and adore the spirit of me, who am Queen of all Witcheries.

There shall ye assemble, ye who are fain to learn all sorcery, yet have not yet won its deepest secrets: to these will I teach things that are yet unknown. And ye shall be free from slavery; and as a sign that ye are really free, ye shall be naked in your rites; and ye shall dance, sing, feast, make music and love, all in my praise. For mine is the ecstasy of the spirit and mine also is joy on earth; for my Law is Love unto all Beings.

Keep pure your highest ideal; strive ever toward it; let naught stop you or turn you aside. For mine is the secret door which opens upon the Land of Youth; and mine is the Cup of the Wine of Life, and the Cauldron of Cerridwen, which is the Holy Grail of Immortality.

I am the Gracious Goddess, who gives the gift of joy unto the heart. Upon earth, I give the knowledge of the spirit eternal; and beyond death, I give peace, and freedom, and reunion with those who have gone before. Nor do I demand sacrifice, for behold I am the Mother of All Living, and my love is poured out upon the earth.

Hear ye the words of the Star Goddess, she in the dust of whose feet are the hosts of heaven; whose body encircleth the Universe; I, who am the beauty of the green earth, and the white Moon among the stars, and the mystery of the waters, and the heart's desire, call unto thy soul. Arise and come unto me.

For I am the Soul of Nature, who giveth life to the universe; from me all things proceed, and unto me must all things return; and before my face, beloved of gods and mortals, thine inmost divine self shall be unfolded in the rapture of infinite joy.

Let my worship be within the heart that rejoiceth, for behold: all acts of love and pleasure are my rituals. And therefore let there be beauty and strength, power and compassion, honour and humility, mirth and reverence within you.

And thou who thinkest to seek for me, know thy seeking and yearning shall avail thee not, unless thou know this mystery: that if that which thou seekest thou findest not within thee, thou wilt never find it without thee.

For behold, I have been with thee from the beginning; and I am that which is attained at the end of desire.

- Spring -

FIRST LIGHT

Look to the east
Laying first light upon the pearly sky
In the motionless dawn
Beginning the beginning
Of still green leaves
Streets washed with silence
And jewelled echoes
It will not last long
And yet it has always been
And endures forever
Every moment the shapes are altering
And what speeds to the night
Speeds to the dawn
Before anyone is up
There are presences walking
Only animals and birds see them
On their royal passage
Smiling hand in hand
With gold and silver crowns
All down in the valley the magic path
Turns into a railway line
The choir of trees
Is dusted with mortality
The eternal dissolves in time
As dawn becomes day

CONSERVATION APPEAL

Help save an endangered species - Homo Sapiens.
Please everyone, consider this appeal.
Recall the extinction of the dinosaurs,
Don't let the poor Homo get the same raw deal.

He isn't very good or very clever;
But then, he's not been here for all that long,
He might evolve some day to be much better,
If nuclear madness doesn't end his song.

His acts are even dafter than the lemming's,
His habits are much filther than the pig's.
He hasn't got the sense to stop polluting
The very Mother Earth in which he digs.

But yet there's something there about the creature,
Some little spark of far-off heaven's fire,
That makes it seem a pity he should perish,
Doomed by his own blind green and false desire.

He cannot leap like antelope or salmon,
Or like the condor soar into the blue.
The flower that he crushes is more lovely,
A dog's heart is more faithful and more true.

He thinks that he's the crown of all creation,
This cruellest predator that Earth e'er spawned!
And yet, and yet, you know, there must be something.
That Gaia meant when evolution dawned.

Somehow, some way, the Gods must want old Homo
(Though he's not indispensable, of course);
But still there's some place for him in the Cosmos
that can't be filled by bird or tree or horse.

So pray let's think about his conservation,
Ere his own folly makes it all too late.
Help save an endangered species, Homo sapiens.
Don't let him share Tyrannosaurus' fate!

July, 1982

SPRING NIGHT

Slivery flutes in a woodland glade
Sing to a plashing stream.
Elf and fay, on this night of May,
Are hailing the full Moon's gleam.

Owls are calling one to another
In trees that are newly green.
By the silver light of their goddess-mother
The fairy revels are seen.

With elfin wings and floating hair,
And feet that leave no trace,
Over the bracken and round the trees
They glide to their trysting-place.

Bluebell and celandine blossom there,
Pale by the moonbeams' light.
Windflowers cover the earth that was bare
Through the long winter night.

Now is the Maytime, now is the spring,
And Green Jack's children play.
Revel they keep, while humans sleep,
Till the first faint dawn of day.

May, 1978

THE WITCHES' CREED

The golden Sun, king of the morning,
The silver Moon, queen of the night,
Enlighten our destiny's pathway,
Made up of the dark and the bright.

Mysterious water and fire,
The earth and the wide-ranging air,
By hidden quintessence we know them,
And will and keep silent and dare.

The birth and rebirth of all nature,
The passing of winter and spring,
We share with the life universal,
Rejoice in the magical ring.

Four times in the year the Great Sabbat
Returns, and the witches are seen
At Lammas and Candlemas dancing,
On May Eve and old Halloween.

When day-time and night-time are equal,
When Sun is at greatest and least,
The four lesser Sabbats are summoned,
Again witches gather in feast.

Thirteen silver moons in a year are,
Thirteen is the coven's array.
Thirteen times at Esbat make merry,
For each golden year and a day.

Let power be passed down the ages,
To and fro between female and male,
Each century unto the other
Retelling the wonderous tale.

When drawn is the magical circle,
By sword or athame* of power,
Its compass between the two worlds lies,
In Land of the Shades for that hour.

This world has no right then to know it,
And world of beyond will tell naught,
When oldest of Gods are invoked there,
And the Great Work of Magick is wrought.

The staff and the cauldron display it,
The secret of sire and dame,
The nature of things universal,
On earth and in heaven the same.

For two are the mystical Pillars,
That stand at the gate of the shrine,
And two are the Powers of Nature,
The forms and the forces divine.

The dark and the light in succession,
The opposites each unto each,
Shown forth as a God and a Goddess,
Even so do our ancestors teach.

By night he's the wild wind's rider,
The Horn'd One, the Lord of the Shades,
By day he's the King of the Woodland,
The life of the green forest glades.

She is youthful or old as she pleases,
She sails the torn clouds in her barque,
The bright silver lady of midnight,
The crone that weaves spells in the dark.

The Master and Mistress of Magick,
They dwell in the deeps of man's mind,
Immortal and ever-renewing,
With power to free or to bind.

So drink the good wine to the Old Gods,
And dance and make love in their praise,
Till Elphame's fair land shall receive us
In peace at the end of our days.

And Do What You Will be the challenge,
So be it in Love that harms none,
For this is the only commandment.
By Magick of old, be it done!

1974

THE CRY

Across the world the mad mobs bay for war.
Will no good spirit seal that dreadful door?
Were humans made for nothing more than this?
To grasp at joy as fleeting as a kiss,
Then wake one day to find the end has come,
All music deadened by the soldiers' drum?
Let it not be, O holy Mother Earth!
Not without hope let new life come to birth,
And flowers bloom upon ruined wall
Once shattered by the screaming missiles' fall.
To you man's spirit cries, O Womb of Life!
Love is your silent answer, ending strife;
Beauty your evidence, eternally.
When will man look and listen, and be free?

APRIL SONG

We see the starry celandines
And hear the chaffinch sing,
And thank the Gods that have spared us
To know another Spring.

The sun's sweet warmth is in the breeze
And golden on the hill.
In every hedge the buds unfold,
And softly flows the rill.

The catkins dance upon the bough
And deck the willow tree,
While overhead the sky is blue
As far as eye can see.

How once again the Green Man's mouth
Has breathed the breath of life,
Again the Goddess blessed the earth,
In spite of hate and strife.

And when we walk the woodland path
There still are songs to sing.
So thank the Gods that have spared us
To know another spring!

AFTER CHERNOBYL

The Sun and the Moon stood still in the sky.
To watch the grief of the world go by.
And each unto the other did say:
"What can we do but weep and pray?"
A sea wave whispered upon the shore,
Of the days that were and are no more,
When all the winds blew free and wild
Across the mountains undefiled.
A lichen grew on an old grey stone,
And spoke to the wind that made its moan:
"Go tell the Moon, go tell the Sun,
I shall be here when all is done.
I was the first, I am the last
To grow when the grief of the world is past."
But "Wrath, wrath" cried the wave of the sea,
And "Anger" moaned the wind in the tree.
Then every other voice did cease,
When the voice of Earth Herself said "Peace."

HOMAGE TO PAN

Homage to the Great God Pan!
Ere aeonic Time began
Marching its slow caravan,
Swift the dance of primal dawn,
When the music of the faun,
Sevenfold in melody,
Echoed cosmic ecstasy.

Long and long the years have passed,
And the sky is overcast
With a cloud of dreams foredone,
Thus have blotted out the sun.
Shattered is the statue's grace,
Stained the marble of its face,
And in ugly vesture stand
All the grey slaves of the land.

Yet there is a secret clime,
Out of space and out of time,
(So the stones of long ago
In the moonlight whisper low,
When the night-winds gently thrill
Through the grasses on the hill),
When all things are wild and free
To be what e'er they want to be.
There doth rise the mystic mountain,
There doth spring the living fountain,
There the silver roebuck leaps
In the enchanted forest deeps,

There within the scented groves,
Satyrs consummate their loves,
And its shining trees are seen
Clothed with an eternal green.

We may find it, if we try,
In the blinking of an eye,
Or may seek long years in vain,
Down the roads of earthly pain,
Once at last to leap and run
From the shadow to the sun.
Where the hoary stone,
Stands upon the upland lone,
Wisdom of an elder day
Waits a heart-beat's breath away.

Honour to the Hornéd Pan!
He it is, since time began,
Piping music of the spheres,
Thrilling beyond mortal ears
Through the spaces of the stars,
Through all earthly bolts and bars,
Calling us from our despond
To infinity beyond,
Where eternal visions gleam,
Fairer than the fairest dream.
When the wild winds rejoice,
Nature echoes back his voice,
And the shape of every tree
Whispers of eternity.

Life and love and death must reel
As the spokes of the great wheel,
Still the music sweet and fond,
Shrilling yet, "Beyond – beyond!"
Sings the last hierogamy,
Past the bounds of earth and sky.

Io! Io! Aegipan!
Laughing yet at mortal ban,
Laughing as a great god can,
Within the stars' bright river ran
Shining through his fingers' span –
Glory to the Hornéd Pan!

January, 1974

THE REDEVELOPMENT

The old house vanished in a dusty cloud,
Its secrets scattered to the winds of air.
Whether its dwellers humble were or proud,
They are forgotten, and its walls stand bare.

Soon the last fragment's gone. The raw earth gapes.
The loud-voiced, sun-bronzed builders have moved in.
Now by their hands arise new-fangled shapes,
New bricks, fresh concrete, motors' roaring din.

A new room grows, where once in the same place
Those others dwelt, who lived and loved and died,
Who came there young, grew old, perhaps found grace.
With new hope now who comes here to reside?

So turns the wheel of time; the cycle runs
For houses, years and galaxies of suns.

THE SONG OF THE ZODIAC

With curling horn, the Ram of the Stars,
Decked in the blaze of blood-red Mars,
Bearing above him the golden sun,
Sets the Zodiac's course to run.
Power and beauty, the Bull of earth,
Led by the emerald Goddess of mirth,
Rears his majestic horns on high
To the silver Moon, the Queen of the sky.
Two gay children, frolicing, dancing
Light as air or a sunbeam's glancing,
The Twins go laughing at Time and Age,
Forever young and forever sage.
Out of a pool that reflects the Moon
Rises the Crab at the summer's noon,
When dreaming lies the mystic sea,
Where treasure and strange secrets be.
The Lion shakes his fiery mane,
The Sun burns down on hill and plain.
In alchemy of wealth untold,
The harvest fields are living gold.
The green-clad Lady of the earth,
Virgin although she giveth birth,
Walks in the dim, dewed fields of morn,
Bearing an ear of ripened corn.
Mid dark and day hang the balanced Scales,
While the rising wind of autumn wails,
And the reddened leaves go dancing light,
And Fate gives victory to the night.
Now death is in the Scorpion's sting,

But life is on the Eagle's wing,
And dark the deep where hidden lies
The Serpent of love's mysteries.
The jolly Centaur bends his bow,
And lets the fiery arrow go,
While thunderous his hoofbeats' sound
Echoes the wild hills around.
The shaggy Goat of horned Pan,
The winter's longest night began;
But glowed among his frosty stars
The ruby of exalted Mars.
And evermore the torrent roars
That out the Water-Bearer pours.
The stream of life through star and earth
Flows to replenish every dearth.
Two Fish with scales of jewel sheen,
In twilight deeps of water seen,
Like image in a poet's dream,
Now, swim, now hide, within the stream.
So Sun and Moon their starry track
Journey around the Zodiac,
And sages old in symbols tell
This their magic circle's spell.

POP SONG

When the stars go out and it's the dark of night
If you put out the light and then put out the light
You can't put it back

Oh oh
Sorry 'bout that
Yes I'm sorry 'bout that
'Cause you can't put it back
And everything that lives is holy
Holy
Everything that lives is holy

Up in the Andes where the air is thin
Where Che Guevara's ashes are blowing in the wind
I heard that condor's ghost say Listen son
When you get that power from the mouth of a gun
You can't put it back

Oh oh
Sorry 'bout that
Yes I'm sorry 'bout that
'Cause you can't put it back
And everything that lives is holy
Holy
Everything that lives is holy

A mountain is just like a grain of sand
What either one's doing there we don't understand
Everything and every other thing is linked
And the forty-seventh species just became extinct
And you can't put it back

Oh oh
Sorry 'bout that
Yes I'm sorry 'bout that
'Cause you can't put it back
And everything that lives is holy
Holy
Everything that lives is holy

When I heard the man say I'd just like to explain
We lost a nuclear warhead off the coast of Spain
Don't know how it happened maybe it was in fun
So you'd better just forget it 'cause there's nothing to be done
And we can't put it back

Oh oh
Sorry 'bout that
Yes I'm sorry 'bout that
'Cause we can't put it back
And everything that lives is holy
Holy
Everything that lives is holy

When I hear that spokesman the way that I feel
I sure would like to put a spoke in his wheel
The way he tells you lady there's nothing I can do
Your father was expendable your son is too
But I can't put it back

Oh oh
Sorry 'bout that
Yes I'm sorry 'bout that
'Cause I can't put it back
And everything that lives is holy
Holy
Everything that lives is holy

April, 1975

THE RETURN

There's a voice on the wind,
Of the Old Gods returning.
There's a light and a flame
Of the witch-fires burning.
Locked were the gateways
Of loving and laughter,
And hidden the keys
For long centuries after.
Now good that was evil
For better is bartered.
No more shall the body
Of Eros be martyred.
The call of the pipe
And the throb of the drum,
The dance of the Sabbat -
Their hour has come!
For Fate is a spiral
That's turning and spinning;
Now we rise, now we fall,
Now we're losing, now winning.
And Life is a river,
That flows through the stars,
All footprints effacing,
Down-breaking all bars.
So that which has been
Shadows that which shall be,
As lie the dead leaves
Round the new-budding tree.

GAIA IN SPRING

The woods are starred with wild anemones,
The blossom of the gorse is burning bright,
The wind sough through the pines like angry seas,
And all the spring is moving into light.

Where tractor's wheels have riven up the earth
The breezes bear the scent of it away,
To mingle with the yellow catkins' mirth
And float across the immemorial clay.

This earth so old, so new and ever young,
Ancestral, bearing yet the greenest leaf,
Gaia, of you the song be ever sung
Of magic that assuages every grief.

Yours the immortal planetary joy
No death can conquer and no war destroy.

April, 1983

THE HORN

Deep down in the woods forlorn
I heard the calling of a horn;
And unto me it seemed to say,
Come and find the secret way

To wondrous things of old -
Moon of silver, sun of gold,
And the elemental powers,
Earth, the mother of the flowers,

And the dancing of the rain
O'er the city and the plain;
Rushing winds on hilltop high,
Evening breeze and owl's cry,

Scented smoke and golden spark
Of the flame that lights the dark.
In the elemental things
Hear the beat of spirit wings.

At the core of things doth lie
A great heart of mystery;
Eightfold are the ways thereto.
Learn with love the rites to do

Unto Them, that timeless stand
In the unseen, ancient land.
Hold the vision and the dream,
Though in murk ye lose the gleam

Of the Star of magic might,
Clouded in the world's dark night.
Elder wisdom sayeth sooth,
The true dream shall come to truth.

Through the woods the elf-note rang,
Echoed in the heart, and sang
Of a book of mysteries,
Closed unto the worldly wise,

That wind doth read and earth descry,
And so may man with inward eye.

LIFE

To what enigma do these words allude,
But life's true image and similitude?
A veil of twilight over a lost world, stir
A furious army with bright flags unfurled.

A poison serpent in a bowl of jade,
A splendid titan trembling and afraid.
The lurid lightning of a gathering storm,
A torrent trapped and frozen into form.

An argent argosy of gallant ships,
A spectre walking in the sun's eclipse.
A magic plant that springs up in the night,
A dance that circles for the gods' delight.
Weave words for ever, 'tis but shadow show.
Pass beyond words, and life itself shall know.

WIDDERSHINS

I curse you against the sun,
I curse you against the moon.
So may the spell be done,
And fall upon you soon.

Back on your evil head
Fall the lies you have spoken.
The arrow you have sped
Shall fall back broken.

Into your own false heart
The splintered shaft shall lodge,
Although you play your part
With shift and cunning dodge.

By night when owls cry
Under the waning moon,
Her sickle in the sky
Is sharp for you soon.

The fool who calls on Fate
Shall deathly echoes hear,
Unloosing from Her gate
The hounds of fear.

Undying as the wind
And swift as thought,
You leave them not behind,
They cannot be bought.

In all Earth is not room
To lose their footsteps fell.
They hunt you to your doom,
The red-eared hounds of hell.

Of your own poison die,
Corrupt and rotten.
Your grave unhonoured lie,
Your name forgotten.

REINCARNATION

Who knows what houses of flesh have builded for me,
Or in what lairs I have lain in space and time?
What corridors of chaos I have wandered,
What torches led me? Who knows?

The eye ever-open, unperceived and perceiving,
The scarab sun at the nadir of night;
And those lively otherwhere wraiths
Who haunt the ancestral crossroads of my blood.

AN UNSOLVED PROBLEM OF PSYCHIC RESEARCH

There was a young lady named Freeman
Who had an affair with a demon.
She said that his cock
Was as cold as a rock -
Now, what in the hell could it be, man?

BETWEEN THE AGES

In the shadow of their arbitrary norm,
Upreared like the Pisan tower,
The much too many cloud with their breaths
The strong sun and the vital moon,
Whose fluent rays the wise rocks drink like wine.
Their buildings are a foolish message
Scribbled upon the horizon.

Shall these insistient mouths, earth-crawling grubs,
Ripen into chrysalids?
Or shall no change but that of the phoenix
Fledge them to the wide air?

The floundering Age of the Fishes,
An enormous, lugubrious monster,
Is cast up, dying,
On the shores of the Great Sea,
The mother of all forms,
Whose dark primordial deep
Gave birth to time itself.

Now rocks a new cradle,
Of a baby secretly born
To the Prince of the Powers of Air.
Sportively the snakes of lightning
Dart their forked tongues to hiss his name,
In sibilant prophecies
Whispered to the four winds

RESURRECTION

Before the spring, the Sun calls to the Earth;
A soundless voice on the wind,
Of the bright Sun-Child.
The stones hear and listen,
The trees stir in their sleep.

The seeds in the earth have knowledge, and live;
And the roots down in the ground are stirred by the rain,
Respond, and know its touch of love.
And the old, old trees,
Twisted at angles, gnarled like faces,
Old goblins of the wood,
Dream of their summer shade, and a shaft of joy
In the thin ray to them, of the springtime sun.

And the dead wood, white with many seasons,
Riddled and run through with lives of small creatures,
Greened with lichen, mossy, bleached like bone,
Finds and feels even yet the ghost of life.
The grass, sanctified by lovers,
Pushes up again its gay green blade.

The mud dissolves the crystals of the frost;
The gems of winter vanish, back to their treasury,
The snow that hid in the hollows.

The young green points of buds, imperceptible
Save to the eye sharpened with searching,
Peep out of the old wood, where the secret sap
Has found the lifting of life, to flow again,
Driven by the pulse of the earth's heart.

Soon there will be flowers, small, triumphant,
Up through the mould, unfolding to the light.
Now, only catkins, leaping like lambs' tails,
Yellow with pollen; arching their furry backs,
Spitting kitten defiance, in the name of living,
Every year, every round of the wheel!

Behold them, knowing heralds
Of the clean dying and to earth returning,
Entering into the maze of resurrection,
Coming forth by day, in the dawn of the day,
In the spring of the year.

WE THE ENCHANTED

O Mighty Pan, whose pipes within the wood
Sound through the leaves of summer's sunlit noon,
Of man and nature art thou understood
By Sabbat fires beneath the wandering moon.

Shrive us of sorrow in thy melody;
Of time and fortune loosen thou the bonds.
The heavy world is but the mask of thee,
Whose eyes look out between the leafy fronds.

Save us, O Pan, and mostly from ourselves;
Our eyes light-dazzled can but darkness see.
The blithe wake-world of angels and of elves,
We, the enchanted, think a dream to be.

THE PAGAN

Oh, morris bells, ring out your peals,
For I'm not born to wear high heels!
My church shall be by the standing stone,
Where a gay ghost pipes on a flute of bone.

And may I live as a pagan free,
With no commandment's chain on me,
Save those the Wiccan Rede fulfil:
'AN IT HARM NONE, DO WHAT YE WILL'

The greenwood echoes the thrush's song.
The cuckoo calls, all summer long.
The voice of wind in the aged trees
Holds wisdom of far centuries.

Whatever the ill that Man may wreak,
By sound and silence, the Old Ones speak.
The pageants of Love and Beauty pass.
The mirror of Hate is a shattered glass.

So let the world grow crabbed and old,
Building itself a tomb of gold.
Mine be the joys that shall remain,
Of life and love, in the sun and rain.

- SUMMER -

THE WITCH'S BALLAD

Oh, I have been beyond the town,
Where nightshade black and mandrake grow,
And I have heard and I have seen
What righteous folk would fear to know!

For I have heard, at still midnight,
Upon the hilltop far, forlorn,
With note that echoed through the dark,
The winding of the heathen horn.

And I have seen the fire aglow,
And glinting from the magic sword,
And with the inner eye beheld,
The HornÈd One, the Sabbat's lord.

We drank the wine, and broke the bread,
And ate it in the Old One's name.
We linked our hands to make the ring,
And laughed and leaped the Sabbat game.

Oh, little do the townsfolk reck,
When dull they lie within their bed!
Beyond the streets, beneath the stars,
A merry round the witches tread!

And round and round the circle spun,
Until the gates swung wide ajar,
That bar the boundaries of the earth
From faery realms that shine afar.

Oh, I have been and I have seen
In magic worlds of Otherwhere.
For all this world may praise or blame,
For ban or blessing nought I care.

For I have been beyond the town,
Where meadowsweet and roses grow,
And there such music did I hear
As worldly-righteous never know.

GLASTONBURY TOR

A mighty mound of earth, a mystic hill.
Above, the great wheel of the stars is turning.
Around, the land of Avalon lies still,
Girt with the Zodiac of ancient learning.
Hermes Thrice-Greatest here his law can show,
For that which is above is so below.

But now the wild wind with whirling cloak
Dances a magic circle round the Tor,
The giant pagan spirits to invoke,
And Gwynn ap Nudd is riding as of yore.
His herald voice within the tower cries
The secret semblance of the earth and skies.

Where points that lonely tower to the stars,
Past, present, future, all are blent in one.
The portal of the Otherworld unbars
Amid the apple-garths of Avalon,
And where the rays of dawning sun have kissed,
Merlin is walking, in the morning mist.

About and roundabout about the spirals wind,
The hidden crypt is resonant with song,
While in and out the magic paths are twined,
Weaving a spell to right the ancient wrong,
Finding the secret centre of the maze
Where burns a fire to set the world ablaze.

August, 1980

NATURA NATURANS

Who perceives the white diamond
Of light beyond light,
The gateway of the Goddess
Between Her dark thighs,
The right and left of the world?
Where dark and bright
Are mingled and one,
Babes of one womb,
And from the inmost love of Her body come.

And who the galaxy
Of star-bright seed perceives,
The impulse of might
To move and waken, and start the throb of time
In primal Night?
She of the left hand, the sinister,
The dark foundress, the upholder of all.
Hers is the earth of all roots,
And the secret waters
Of the first fountain,
Where the seas quench their thirst.

YE OLDE MAYE GAME

(or "Lost in the Celtic Twilight")

O, sorrow's on the petals of the rose!
What was, is not. And past hath future been.
For who would think that a man's own false teeth
Would bite him in the arse on Halloween?

O fires of spring and mattress eke alike,
My love lies dead, and lustily doth snore.
For some fell toad the Sabbat wine did spike,
And cracked her sacred crown upon the floor.

Sawdust to sawdust, in a four-ale bar,
Hell is afoot, and none shall sleep in peace,
So place it in the cauldron and depart.
The egg is hatched, and crows the cockatrice!

CITY ON THE COAST

Nirvana and Samsara are one
Said the stone to the water
Nirvana and Samsara are one
Said the wind to the tree

But whom do we tell it to
To me to you
To the old man with the dead cigarette
And the woman with the dead red lips
And a dog on a lead

The sun and the rain are mercy
We do not perceive them so
Because we wear clothes
Everywhere we go

Beyond is near
Far is near
And near is far
The other side of the galaxy
Is like the lining of a coat
The dark side of the moon
Is hidden silver
Polished by the winds of space

And sea wave lace
Frills round the island
In rotting wood is a city
Full of dwellers in dark lanes

53

We too have our habitations
All dressed up naked on the wheel
Perceive the function of the wrathful deities
In the night with the auras of flame
Earth is a wheel that brings the sun
Plants with small green hands
Tear the city apart
With no one to admire the ruins
Only the Buddha-Form is left.

9th May, 1975

THE ACCURSED

Whene'er I see the world changed for the worse,
A good old-fashioned copper-bottomed curse
Rises within! Now may a murrain light
On all the crass thick-headed whelps of night,
The sly exploiters and the greedy clowns
Who foul our woods with rubbish from their towns,
Disgorge their oil into our sickened seas
And mix their stenches with the summer breeze,
Who turn the earth to wasteland grim and sad.
May moonlight split their skulls and drive them mad -
Now stay, you angry witch! Just hold it steady,
Aren't they ensorcelled and accursed already?
Lost in illusions of materialism,
They need no curse. Their need is exorcism!

THE BROOMSTICK FLIGHT

Widdershins in waning moon,
Round about the cauldron go.
Call upon the HornÈd One,
By black candles' flickering glow.

Here in Witchdom's secret place,
Where between the worlds we meet,
Do the deed without a name,
Drink elixir deadly sweet.

You the Pentagram upright,
Limbs outstretching to embrace.
He the Pentagram reversed,
Shows the HornÈd Master's face.

Feel the broomstick ëtween your legs,
Flying high in ecstasy,
Soaring through the midnight air
Over land and over sea.

Till at last the morning star
Rises in the dawn-flushed sky.
Then enwrapped in peaceful dream,
Resting in our beds we'll lie.

February, 1997

KING OF THE WOOD

Greenwood God, we thee invoke,
Spirit of the mighty oak,
As we stand beneath thy tree,
May thy blessing on us be.

In its leaves a mystic voice
Bids the pagan heart rejoice.
May we feel the living power
Flowing from thee in this hour,

Spirit of the life of earth
Through the round of death and birth.
Ever as the year is turning
Keep the secret flame a-burning.

Circle round the witches' fire,
Heat the cauldron of desire.
Here beneath the windy sky
Rear the sacred antlers high,

Dance and stamp with cloven hoof
Underneath the starry roof.
Thee the trees and wild things bless,
Glory to the wilderness!

Hearken to the pagan cry,
Trees shall live when cities die,
Four winds blow their dust away,
Rain shall turn it into clay,

And the arching rainbow's sheen
Lend the earth its emerald green.
Thus it was before man came,
And shall ever be the same,

Through all mortal things that be,
One immortal destiny.
This we know, beneath thy tree.
One with Nature, blessed be!

THE MOTHER DEEP

Behold within the glittering sea
The moon-led tides of mystery.
Its water swirls upon the sand
Uncannily like outstretched hand,
Grasping its hunger to assuage,
With sentience of timeless age.
Strange forms within its purple deep
Move like some phantasm of sleep,
While countless creatures spin and spire,
Glowing with phosphorescent fire.
Upon one far forgotten morn,
Out of its waters life was born,
And while the aeons slowly passed,
Across the land life was spread at last,
The monstrous and the beautiful,
The shell, the lichen and the skull.
Yet deep within all memory
There echoes the ancestral sea.

June, 1998

THE BALLAD OF SIR ROUGHCHOPS

A knight of old, so brave and bold,
Sir Roughchops was his name,
And carrying his trusty spear,
He sought for knightly fame.

One summer evening he rode forth,
All armoured for the fray,
Till in a valley deep he found
A darksome wooded way.

On either side the bushes grew,
Till past a little spring
He saw the entrance to a cave.
Said Roughchops, "Here's a thing!"

"Surely within this cavern dark
Adventure waits for me?
I'll get my weapon ready raised,
And go inside and see."

A witch's cauldron there he found,
That bubbled, stewed and simmered,
Upon a magic bonfire's glow,
That through the twilight glimmered.

And then the wicked witch herself
To Roughchops whispered, "Sir,
You're just the man I'm looking for
To give this pot a stir."

So Roughchops, to oblige the witch,
Being a courteous knight,
Stuck his stiff weapon well inside,
And stirred with all his might.

But oh, alas, that wicked witch
On Roughchops laid a spell!
He stirred and stirred and could not stop,
Though why he could not tell.

Till with a last tremendous stir
The cauldron overset,
And flooded all the cave around
With streams both warm and wet.

When Roughchops drew his weapon out,
It looked all limp and weak,
Whereat the knight was so amazed,
That he could scarcely speak.

The evil hag with cackling laugh
Off on her broomstick shot,
And Roughchops with a thoughtful air
Rode back to Camelot.

Now what black art was wrought on him,
A secret must remain;
But strange to say, he straight set out
To find that cave again!

MIDSUMMER AT GLASTONBURY

I
Evening:

A golden Moon arising from the mist
Rays down enchantment upon Avalon.
As in the dream of antique alchemist,
The Great Work's opposites are joined in one.

By sunset light the pilgrims climb the Tor,
Whose roofless tower points to infinity.
They whisper tales of legendary lore,
Seeing the hills in sacred trinity.

One round green hill the Sangraal's bowl recalls.
Another bears a thorn bent by the wind.
The third, the Tor's steep side, where glowing falls
The last red gleam the sunset gleams behind.

The spirit of the vision spreads its wings,
Invisible and soundless, o'er the sky.
Vibrant and numinous, the holy things,
In pageant sensed unseen, are passing by.

Inscrutable, that face of lunar gold
Sees the illumined Mysteries unfold.

II
Morning:

A sea of mist that rolls across the land
Makes islands of the hills. The pearly sky
Clouds like a crystal cradled in the hand,
And songbirds greet the dawn with muted cry.

A sweet breath rises from the summer fields,
With flowers full of light-reflecting gems
Of dew the night mysteriously yields,
Crowning each weed with wondrous diadems.

The hedges garlanded with wild rose
Lead where the gnarled and secret oak-trees stand,
Silent and hidden, where was once the close
Of Druid way across the magic land.

Above the Tor a gold-entinctured light
Shines through the veil, affirming day begun,
And once again in triumph over Night
Has rested here the chariot of the Sun.

With light that grows and wanes, the Great Wheel turns.
The inmost secret flame, unchanging burns.

June, 1983

CONGRESSUS CUM DEMONAE

Beloved Incubus, Belazarak,
Come, come to me, out of the midnight black.
Bring me the magick weapon I desire,
That enters in like ice and leaves like fire.

Belazarak, now come, now come to me,
And consummate the Nuptiae Sabbati!
Fill my unholy graal with demon seed,
That the Great Work in ecstasy may breed.

By mystery of Congressus Subtilis,
Open the door that leads to secret bliss.
Embrace me by the magick starlight's gleam,
And be my lover in the realms of dream.

March, 1997

THE FOUR AIRTS

The first light puts its fingers through the curtains.
Outside, a cockerel shouts about the dawn.
A touch of cold air comes from the crimson east.
On the hills, the sere grass shakes with it.
In the city, paper blows among the streets.
There is a stir of movement out of sleep,
While the Sun opens his great eye.
The night-shaded houses bathe in air,
The trees wave their arms in it,
And all the leaves dance with secret delight.

Then the Sun swings up, a sure hero,
Young while the aeons pass,
And crowned with unearthly gold.
He climbs to his throne in the south
At the white noon.
The Earth communes with him,
Heated with his fire,
Uplifting the hills of her enticing body,
The perfume of her valleys and her woods;
Calling him down again to her scented darkness.
The rose of their love flushes over the west,
And darkens into the dun veils of twilight,
The cloaks of her sorcery,
The mists from her cauldron of the sea.

A far-off song echoes from the river of Time,
And the doors of the Otherworld open.
The surety of the horizons is gone.

Faint silver witch-light plays round the crest of the hills.
The city marks itself out with strings of lamps,
Preserving its identity
Against the inflowing dark.
The incantation of sleep
Mingles with its rhythms,
And those who wake are wary and alone.
Only the Moon's children run softly to midnight trysts,
And know the thrill through the earth, from the black north.

LOVE SONG

In the deep midnight
Move to my side
Love's a true thing love
Why should it hide

Hearing the footsteps
Pass in the street
Kiss me and hold me
Feel my heart beat

Give me your sweet love
Love's a true thing
Fair as the moonrise
Warm as the spring

Run like the river
Fall like the rain
Love's a true thing love
Pleasure and pain

Grow like a flower
Under the snow
Love's a true thing love
Let it be so

1975

SUMMER NIGHT'S RAIN

A summer night's rain,
And the streets are all gleaming.
With broken reflections
The puddles are teeming.

The red and the green
Of the traffic-lights' glow
Are shining like jewels
That flash to and fro.

The rain-laden wind
Is fragrant and soft.
The scent of the woodlands
It carries aloft.

Perfumes it bears,
O'er the city's dark streets,
On town-dwellers windows
Disturbingly beats.

See all the raindrops
Like fairies are dancing!
Their rhythm half-heard
Is a chorus entrancing;

"Ah, for the wildwood,
The wind and the rain,
And all the green leaves
Down a lost country lane!

The scent of the grass
And the storm-thrush's call,
And the sweet summer rain
Like a blessing o'er all.

What fools men are,
That they see not the pity
To lose all these things
For the noise of a city!"

So sing the raindrops,
So whispers the breeze;
But men fear to listen
To voices like these.

They deafen their ears
With a coin's merry clank,
And deposit their souls
In the vaults of a bank;

Till some empty day,
When they look round afraid,
And know then, too late,
The bad bargain they made.

THE SONG OF THE WEREWOLVES

The grey wolf's skin! The grey wolf's skin!
This is the robe to lap us in.
By the spell of unholy cunning,
Through the dark night the wolves are running.
A wolf by night and a man by day,
And woe to any we meet on the way.
Running light through the leafless trees,
Hear our cry on the midnight breeze,

While the cold white moon shines overhead,
And the peasants hark with shuddering dread.
We are the ones no longer human,
Who run and leap and care for no man.
Serfs by day – now we are free,
Though we be damned for eternity!
In our souls is the dark midnight,
And the mischief moon with her lawless light,

And the Lord of the Forest will we adore,
As the rising winds through the branches roar.
We'll hold high revel in wolfish form,
And howl again to the gathering storm.
How are we strong of fang and claw,
The transformation of ancient awe.
How we run upon four swift feet,
We who walk in the village street,

And bare our heads and bow us low,
When the priest and gentry past us go.

Now the shadowy woods are all around,
And perfumes rise from the wild ground,

And all things are untamed and free,
Timeless and ancient as the sea.
Cry again to the setting moon,
For the red-streaked dawn comes all too soon,
And we can no more revel and leap,
But human wake from our trancéd sleep.
Oh, the grey wolf's skin, the grey wolf's skin
Is the magic robe that we lap us in!

A VISIT TO GLASTONBURY

Now ripening corn waves in the golden fields,
Ragwort stands ready for a witch's wand,
The sun-warmed wind play with the scarlet poppies,
And azure heaven's away on high for ever.

Time to travel away, follow the miles
To the far blue distance, the enchanted hills,
Maybe to meet with Merlin, on the magic island
Arising from the floods of dream and vision.

In dreams, within the hollow hill
I see that august court
Of the presences of Elfin,
Their cloaks and their jewels.
They smile at Time and Fate,
They mock at none.

Stretched out before them is the ancient secret,
Rounded by rivers, shaped by summer fields,
Worked out by wandering ways and wooded hills,
Till the great beasts leap out from the landscape,
Turning their Zodiac, too big to be seen.

Rainclouds forgather over the storied land,
Herded by the wind across Tor and town.
Above the wild gleam of slanted sunlight
O'er Ynis Wytrin writes the Druid name.

THE GATHERING FOR THE ESBAT

O Moon that rid'st the night to wake,
Before the dawn is pale,
The hamadryad in the brake,
The satyr in the vale,

Caught in thy net of shadows,
What dreams hast thou to show?
Who treads the silent meadows
To worship thee below?

The patter of the rain is hushed,
The wind's wild dance is done;
Cloud-mountains ruby-red were flushed
About the setting sun;

And now beneath thine argent beam
The wildwood standeth still.
Some spirit of an ancient dream
Breathes from the silent hill.

Witch-Goddess Moon, thy spell invokes
The Ancient Ones of night.
Once more the old stone altar smokes,
The fire is glimmering bright.

Scattered and few thy children be,
Yet gather we unknown,
To dance the old round merrily
About the time-worn stone,

We ask no heaven, we fear no hell,
Nor mourn our outcast lot,
Treading the mazes of a spell
By priests and men forgot.

- AUTUMN -

THE LONG MAN OF WILMINGTON

As years and centuries go by,
The Long Man watches silently,
While over him cloud shadows pass
In fleeting shapes across the grass.

Upon the hill-top overhead
Lie barrows of the unknown dead.
A distant skylark sings on high,
Melody falling from the sky,

And cottage gardens lie at ease
Among the murmuring of bees.
Within the Priory below
He saw the monks both come and go.

The walls they built to God on high
An open, flower-clad ruin lie.
Yet the Long Man stands stark and still
Against the green grass of the hill.

His dodman's staff in either hand,
He gazes out across the land,
Bearing his message from the past,
The ancient ways shall ever last.

A NIGHT IN THE NEW FOREST

A crescent argent blazoned bright
Upon the sable shield of night,
So shines the moon in heaven's height
Above the wildwood lone.
And cold the nightwind blowing free
Whistles around the withered tree
That used the trysting place to be,
Its trunk bleached white as stone.

On the far road the headlights beam
And pass like phantoms in a dream,
While here the silent starlight's gleam
Recalls time long ago.
Here witches met in olden time,
Away beyond the church bells' chime,
In worship from(?) the ancient prime
That it was death to know.

Ancestral voices fill the skies,
Starlight and witchfire in my eyes,
And echoes of lost centuries
Across this elfin ground.
And here again, in years of war,
They met as they had met before,
To weave the spell they wove of yore
And dance the circle's round.

Stirred by the nightwind stealing by,
The bracken rustles with a sigh.
Deep in the woods an owl's cry
Calls from a distant tree.
This starry night no spectre shows,
No magic flame of bonfire glows;
But all around I feel them close
In ghostly company.

SUCCESS AND FAILURE

All Orders and circles shall fail,
For the results of success are unthinkable.
How terrible if the door of the citadel should fall!
Is it not a fearful thing
If an invocation should invoke?
Or a prayer produce a face in heaven?
For if the Veil should rend,
The nakedness of the world is discovered.
Yet shall there be degrees in failure.
There shall not be darkness without a lamp.
The flame flares and wavers on the walls.
Though it reveal but the stones of the sanctuary,
Its nature is of the unshadowed Light.

HOW GREEN WAS MY OLIVE?

(or "The Chastening Of Charlie")

An Epic Poem, translated from an Ancient Celtic Tradition, and done into verse by A.W. Itch. (The original MS. Was dug up in a Druid urn inscribed "2,000 B.C." It is therefore of unimpeachable authenticity).

This is the tale of Charlie Whim,
Who wanted folks to notice him.
His little heart had one ambition,
He longed to be a Great Magician.

So, as a step to shining fame,
He sought himself a brand new name.
Painful 'twould be to tell you how
He swotted o'er "The Golden Bough",

"Witchcraft Today", "The Book of Signs";
His visage creased with worried lines
Until his sister said, "My dear,
If you go on like this, I fear

You'll get more wrinkles on your face
Than beauty balm can e'er erase.
Just pick one from "The Golden Bough",
And let that be enough for now".

So Charlie did, with magic pin,
And said, "My reign shall now begin.
I'll claim the sovreignty myself,
And gather in much worldly pelf".

For Charlie, strangely to relate,
Although completely consecrate
To higher things than bees-and-honey,
Forever talked and talked of money.

"Now let a sanctuary be made",
Said Charlie, "in this handy glade
Where two streams meet (Whoops! Don't fall in!)
And then our rites we can begin".

A handyman there Charlie had,
A poor, unlettered gipsy lad;
But none the less, some lore had he
Of witches and the Romany.

And greedily did Charlie yearn
To gather all that he could learn,
Or pry, or filch, or ape, or steal,
From what the gipsy could reveal;

Though by and by, the gipsy chal
Perceived that Charlie was no pal.
But leave we this aside, for now
Charlie's prepared to make his bow!

In sumptuous flat, all fresh revealed,
With leopard skins, and lights concealed
In Chinese lamps, and rare perfume
Of joss-sticks burned in every room

(Even the smallest!); there he'd drape
His shoulders with a dashing cape,
While Sis in purple robe stood by –
It was a feast for any eye!

For eyes of all? Well, all save one.
It was a shame to spoil the fun,
But one day came an aged man,
Foredoomed to ruin Charlie's plan.

Questions he asked, right pointedly.
Charlie began to wish that he
had ne'er invited this old fool,
to win him over to his school.

For this old man the world had travelled,
And mysteries strange had oft unravelled.
In witch-lore learned well was he,
In magic and all glamourie.

(But two great faults did him besmutch;
He'd a kind heart, and talked too much).
Our Charlie soon with rage perceived
His grand pretensions weren't believed.

His crown fell off, his throne had crumbled;
In short, our Charlie-boy was rumbled!
"<u>Celtic</u> tradition? Why do you
Then call on Thor? I thought you knew

That Thor's a Scandinavian god?"
Oh, it gave Charlie such a prod!
"<u>That</u> a witch sword? It's Arabic!"
It was enough to make you sick!

"<u>That</u> was dug up from Pompeii?
Well I'd say nineteenth century.
No patina is on the metal,
It's modern as a Woolworths' kettle!"

Charlie and Sis, their faces fell;
They wished the aged man to hell.
Their plans of being top-flight witches
Had run into all sorts of hitches.

But Charlie said, "I've lots of cash.
What we can't rule, then we shall smash!"
And so, with spite and fury fired,
Back to the woods our Charles retired;

And there, enwrapped in thoughts unholy,
He brooded, 'mid the gladioli.
With thwarted spite and anger deep
He seethed just like a compost heap.

From hatred's black and deadly seed
Grew in his heart a poison weed,
And in the dark of one lunation
It burgeoned – a full-blown mutation!

"Aha!" he said, "I've got a plan
Of vengeance on that aged man.
I'll find a likely bit of skirt
That I can train to do him hurt.

Some jade I'll prime to act the part –
Sure, none would do it but a tart,
But she could turn the old fool's brain,
And then come back to me again

With any secrets she could steal –
I'll bring the damned old witch to heel!
He's old and soft and unsuspecting –
I'll show him I don't take rejecting!"

(And as his scheme fell into place,
Our Charlie's wizened, foxy face,
All twisted up with rage and spite,
T'was not a very pleasant sight.)

So Charlie did his fists unclench,
And hied in search of likely wench.
And did he in some clip-joint get her?
Oh, no! His luck was something better.

For Charlie found a splendid pupil,
Quite without any awkward scruple.
A real aristocrat was she,
And entered in the scheme with glee.

Her lovely eyes with malice glistened –
The Guru taught, the Chela listened.
"Fool the old man? And fool his wife?
And do my best to smear his life?

Swear he can trust me? That I'll love!
For we, of course, just rise above
Such morals as some peasant prates,
We two are real Initiates!"

Although her tricks were cheap and shady,
Let's get it straight – she was a lady!
(What's that? You don't believe it? Go,
Look in "Who's Who' – it must be so.

And ever since these things occurred,
"Lady" has been a dirty word).
Down to her desk she sat, and wrote
A pretty little flattering note

To the old man, and spoke him fair;
And his old wife received her there
Within their home, and at their table,
The while she filched all she was able;

Even with swift photography,
Just like a hired private eye!
To learn of witchcraft she besought,
And begged that all she might be taught;

So he within the circle brought her,
To swear good faith before the altar.
And there she tried with might and main
Him to seduce; but all in vain.

Why, was the sage to Venus cold?
No, not at all – just much too old!
(And what was more, his wife and he
Had started scenting treachery).

The old man then she swiftly spurned,
And back to Charlie straight returned.
All hastily they brought the swag in,
And sorted it like Sykes and Fagin.

"You've not got much! Well, never fret,
We'll work it up to something yet.
We'll frame it in a few smart lies,
And publish when the old man dies.

He can't live long; and when he's dead,
How to disprove what we have said?"
(In spite of magic crown and throne,
Charlie was coward to the bone).

So Charlie waited, till the day
He heard the sage had passed away.
Then up he jumped with furious bound,
And whirled his magic sword around!

"Ah, now I'll strike them all with fear –
Oh, damn, there goes the chandelier!
Oh, don't fuss, Sis! It doesn't matter.
He's <u>dead</u> - now let the presses clatter!"

THE SANCTUARY

In the room outlooking on sunset clouds
And dark stiff shapes of towers,
Find the shifting path
Between gliding layers of music.
Timeless the four talismans
Take up their stance at the quarters
Of the focussing circle,
The silent concourse of forces
At the place of convergence.
The invocation of the waiting flames,
The speech of incense,
The parables of weapons,
All alike speak, each in their orders,
To their fellows not shapen
By the carving of sight and touch.
In the five lamps of sense, when the flames
are shaken
By a wind between the worlds,
We find far echoes from the core of light.

DEUS CORNUTUS

As the wheel is turned and the web is spun,
How many names has the Hornéd One?
Great Amoun from the shadowy clime
Of mighty Khem in the long-lost time.
Goatfoot Pan from the sunlit hills
Of Hellas, where the panpipe thrills
Its melody through the leafy grove,
Where the satyrs dance and the centaurs rove.

Then from the pines of the snow-clad north
See Odin's hunt go galloping forth,
On midnight wind that wildly shrieks
Over the barren mountain peaks.
In greenwood hiding the fairy folk,
Glory of Britain, the mighty oak
Shadows a form among the fern,
Shelters the cloaked and antlered Herne.

Through the heat of the forest's noon,
Or by the ray of the rising moon,
Faintly echoes his horn a-calling —
The veil between the worlds is falling.
Janicot of the heath remote
And the merry field of the Sabbat goat,
Where at midnight black the bonfires blaze
And dancers whirl as the piper plays.

Faring far from the ages deep
Where the magical art arose from sleep,
And a nameless god with an antlered head
Loosed on the wall of the cave of dread,
The secret shrine where the dawn-men came
To grave him there by a glimmering flame,
Many the Horns of Honour bore
Down the centuries gone before.
As the wheel is turned and the web is spun,
How many names has the Hornéd One?

May, 1984

THE DOOR

Knockings upon the door of the unknown
Evoke an echoing answer.
A footstep falls in the cloisters of the mind.
The dream tapestries, troubled
By a breeze of other air,
Sway in their shifting patterns,
When day is blind,
And perfumed twilight with dim stars is fair.
Listen to the stream of silence flowing,
That feeds the moat about the Castle,
And laps upon its aeon-builded walls.
The illusion of day has hid that which is there.
Purity has veiled the pure,
And the virtuous have blackened virtue,
And the five senses sealed each the door.
Now knock;
And three times knock,
For the Old One Three-fold,
Who answer gives from earth and sea and air.

COMPUTER BLUES

Sitting on top of a block of flats
Belfry's so clean that there aint no bats
Planned out a tower way up to the sky
Never thought there'd be a tower so high
Suppose one day it should fall down hard
Just like the tower in the Tarot card

Land's sakes
They never make mistakes
Computer emperor computer guru
They got big round tapes and little switches too
Just like faces all looking at you
Giving you computer blues

The letter says man you've got to agree
You owe a million dollars to the Treasury
Don't delay just go on and pay
'Cause computer's all ready to file you away

Land's sakes
They never make mistakes
I got those new computer blues

I went in a shop to get some new clothes
They all said aint got none of those
Big computer says don't stock them no more
Wonderful computer just runs this store

Land's sakes
They never make mistakes
Sell you the computer blues

Wake up in the night about half past two
See those little faces all looking at you
Electronic fortune-tellers all printing out
Like they really know what it's all about

Land's sakes
They never make mistakes
The doctor said man just lie down on the bed
'Cause computer says we've got to cut off your head
You can't stand still you've got to progress
We all want more so we all get less
Get the new computer blues

Computer come putter utter compost stop

1975

THE GOD OF ARIÈGE

Long is the road of years
Back to that cavern dim,
Where on the sacred wall
The cavemen pictured him.
There the old Sorcerer
Dances down centuries,
Through birth and life and death,
For both the gates are his.
Within the hornéd mask
Two ghostly eyes are staring,
Out of the past unknown
To years of future faring.
This is the male, the hero,
To pleasure and to mate,
To stir the womb's dark cauldron
Of She who maketh fate.
Beneath the dim feet dancing
The trodden pathways lie,
Of all the mazes winding,
Of all who love and die.
The gate of life burst open,
That virgin blood doth mark,
Shall bring them resurrection
That went into the dark.
Out of the night of time
The timeless wizard see,
Casting the spell of life
By ancient sorcery.

ATLANTIS

I saw an old land, lost and drowned,
Where songs were sung, long, long ago,
In temples of cyclopean stone,
By altar lamps unearthly glow.

A whole lost world lies buried there,
And knowledge now to us unknown.
The green wave covers all the land,
A sunken wilderness of stone.

Here by ruined temple arch,
Strange creatures of eternal night,
Glide and entwine in fearful shapes,
By eerie phosphorescent light.

Jewels and gold there lie entombed,
And giant bones of ages past,
Until the starry horoscope
In right ray-pattern shines at last.

Then shall the secret be revealed,
And temple doors unlocked by time.
Her children shall their mother know,
And far Atlantis rise sublime.

The Spellers

With words we spin love,
With words we spin hate,
And twenty-six letters
Are weavers of fate.

Many and strange
Are the patterns they weave,
Some blazoning truth,
And some meant to deceive.

Many a testament,
Many a page
Of man's endless book,
From age unto age,

Still he writes on,
His own changing history,
For those who come after
To ponder its mystery.

A sign-posted road,
Or the words on a tomb,
A letter of love,
Or a sentence of doom,

Still twenty-six letters
In words interweaving,
Expressing our joy,
Or voicing our grieving.

Painstaking children
Are striving to spell;
Sages their wisdom
Are seeking to tell;

A leader speaks out
To a listening nation;
A witch whispers low
A weird incantation;

And all of their thoughts
And their voices are heard,
In the charm-woven letters,
The Spell of the Word.

TO ALEISTER CROWLEY

How enigmatic is the face
That looks down from its portrait's place
Atop the bookcase in my room,
Werein your youth's exotic bloom
Of poetry rests side by side
With all you wrote in manhood's pride
Of magick. The half-laughing sage
That you became in your old age,
He too is here. And that new law,
"Do what thou wilt" that shook with awe
And rage so many years ago,
The folk that found it written so.
O Therion, beast self-proclaimed,
And of all men the most ill-famed,
O poet of the golden tongue
Whose verses marvellously sung
Are like a wondrous tapestry
Of bright bejewelled fantasy,
Were you indeed the demon Crowley,
Adept averse of all unholy,
Nefarious, black forbidden things,
Or did you bid us put on wings
To soar beyond this mortal plane
At any cost of shame or pain?
I see in you the high adept
Crying the dawn to souls that slept
And in you too the baser man
That earned the name of charlatan.
Do we have right to shun you still

For pointing us to our True Will?
Your flawed and tragic life is done,
How shall we judge you, Therion?
Not ours the hand that holds the seals
That weigh the told and untold tales
Of mortal life. That must befall
In the vast shadowy Judgement Hall
Of great Osiris. We know not
The end of which we were begot,
Still less of sister or of brother.
Who are we then to judge another?
This much I know, that you availed
To show the Magick Art unveiled,
Your first-sword motto proven sure:
"Perdurabo" - I shall endure.

THE HEAD OF BRAN

Through the opened doors of death and dream,
This I saw, at the edge of the world.
Cleft grey rocks, and water-worn boulders,
Born from the womb of the mother of life,
And thin between are the grass-green blades
Of life in the land of death upspringing.

Come you in, and venture your step
On the earth of the land unearthly.
Tread on nothing, where there is no thing,
See without eyes, and hear the silence.
You have lost your wits, and so ye shall know.

Bring in the tattered and the mad, being dressed rightly
To hear that voice which speaks beyond the voices.
So Beltane fire shall lighten up the dark,
And life and flesh, be to the bleaching bones.

Behold a severed head, most venerate,
And laid with awe upon the lichened stone.
In four streams down, is drying the dark blood.
His eyes are fire of life. O pallid face,
At which man's soul is stricken down in love!
The wind between the world doth stir his hair
And silvern beard, in light of that lost place.
Wonder and pity at the outpoured blood.

Behold this head, the Power of Sacrifice;
For life and death within that place are one.
His speech is borne upon the spectral wind.
O Death and Life in Death, O Ancient One,
Thy words are life, shaped in the stone unhewn;
To move with stillness, grip with open hand.

PRESENCES

Listening to the great elemental voice of the sea,
Speaking in no tongue and all tongues,
While above the clouds are crowding,
Gathering into night and storm,
Who are the watchers of this scene, beside myself?
Whose are the gay indifferent presences
Writhen in cloudrack and outshaped by air?
They feel no chill as I, only exultation.
Their pulse is in the surging of the tide.
They lie silent in stone,
Yet have speech among themselves.
Their life is in shapes and shadows,
We cannot know them
And we to them are equally unheeded.
The mist on the sea is their veil,
Illusory, for they are in no thing,
And so in all things,
They, the presences of life,
Angels and demons both, and gods of faery.
Sometimes for sport they will approach us,
Shaping their powers in clouds or sunlit water,
Looking a sudden face from the bole of a tree,
Or sigil printed on a coloured stone.
The Moon is their lady and ours
And leads their blithe dancing,
As they move invisible, mocking and mastering
The hardness of our world.

LAMENT FOR THE LAND OF KHEM

Where once the horns of great Amoun
Protected Egypt's sovereignty,
The sun upon the desert sand
Shows where the broken columns lie.
The harpers and the trumpeters,
The dancers and the shaven priests,
Their bones are mingled with the dust,
Forgotten like the humble beasts.
How ruthless is the hand of time
That strips the shattered pyramid,
And chokes with sand the labyrinth
Where secrets aeon-old lie hid.
Yet glow the colours on the walls
And still the cavern faces smile,
As if they see the boat of Ra
Serene on the celestial Nile.
And from each stone colossus there
Echoes at dawn a soundless cry,
To hail the pageant of the Gods
Eternal as the sunlit sky.
So great the magic of that land
That we forsaken are of them,
And in the dreamworld yearn to find
The pylon-guarded gates of Khem,
Out of the astral twilight see
The veiled and moon-crowned Isis loom,
And breathe, awakened, lingering there
A scent of spices and perfume.

HERMAPHRODITE PANTHEA

A vision from enchanted realms unknown:
Twin powers male and female, joined in one.
Life's potencies by magic art foreshown;
A miracle conjoined of Moon and Sun.

The breasts of Venus and the loins of Pan,
The antique world knew thee for Goddess-God.
Mystery manifest of woman-man,
Round thee of old the sacred dance we trod.

Perfect thy beauty of the sexes both.
Through cloudy incense-smoke thy deep eyes gaze;
So that we kneel in worship, nothing loth
To do thy will in rites unto thy praise.

THE TAROT TRUMPS

0.

First comes the tattered Fool, the numberless,
Out of the neverland of wonder's guess,
His wild eyes fixed on distances afar.
Does he but dream, or see things as they are?

I.

And next the nimble Juggler with his table.
Full well his art with cunning fingers able
To fool us is. But magic may be sooth,
And all his deepest trick to show us truth.

II.

The Priestess sits before the temple's veil,
With crescent crown, and robe of moonlight pale.
But when we peer within, what do we see?
No temple there but heaven, earth and sea.

III.

Throned in the beauty of the ripening corn,
Rich-robed she sits, a Queen and Empress born.
All art her shadow from most ancient days,
All truest poesy her song of praise.

IV.

Behold the Emperor in armour bright,
With royal sceptre in his hand of might,
Enthroned upon the Stone of Mysteries.
His piercing glance looks forward, strong and wise.

V.

The Hierophant before the world of men
The truth reveals, the Veil lets fall again.
In Egypt and Eleusis hath he been,
And now by sun and now by shadow seen.

VI.

The Lovers gaze upon each others' face,
And choice is made within that moment's space.
Male unto female, complemented, whole;
The Great Work's matter, both in flesh and soul.

VII.

In triumph rides the armoured Charioteer,
And of their own accord his horses steer.
One bright, on dark; but each a noble steed.
The strength of both his chariot doth speed.

VIII.

Justice enthroned displays her sword and scales.
Hers is the Law, that falters not nor fails.
Beyond man's rules, more dreadful and more kind,
Nought can escape her, for she is not blind.

IX.

With cloak and staff he wanders o'er the world,
Though kingdoms fall, and down to dust be hurled.
He passeth by, and where he will doth stay,
The Hidden Master, on his secret way.

X.

Dame Fortune's Wheel forever turns about,
So some rise high, while others are cast out.
We may by wisdom that great wheel discern;
But how to see the Hand that doth it turn?

XI.

Here at first sight doth Strength belie its name,
For an enchanted lion frolics tame.
At beauty's feet he lies at her command,
And lifts his head to lick her virtuous hand.

XII.

Here is upreared the dismal gibbet dark,
Where the Hanged Man doth swing for all to mark,
With mute and stubborn question ominous;
For do we him reproach, or doth he us?

XIII.

A grisly skeleton with scythe-blade bare,
Behold grim Death, the ancient leveller.
There fall before him crownéd heads of kings,
Yet at his feet the flower forever springs.

XIV.

An Angel pouring water into wine,
The emblem we to Temperance assign.
So mingled natures something better prove;
Thus teaches life, and alchemy, and love.

XV.

Here is the Devil, whom the witches call
The Hornéd One, and Eldest God of All.
He will abide, though frowning priests condemn;
For ancient Nature is not ruled by them.

XVI.

A stricken Tower, rent by lightning flash;
Its turrets proud down into ruins crash.
By this we see the mighty works of men
By fire from Heaven are brought low again.

XVII.

Above the earth the Star shines clear and bright,
Showing most fair in depth of darkest night;
While Nature in her unveiled beauty seen,
Pours forth the stream of life from worlds unseen.

XVIII.

A waning Moon that casts illusion round,
'Mid fearful voice of wolf and baying hound.
Her magic here is glamourie and dream,
And things bewitched, that be not what they seem.

XIX.

O lovely Sun, that brightens all the day,
While hand in hand the children dance and play,
Within a garden full of flowers bright,
Naked and innocent beneath your light.

XX.

The dead awake! They rise up and rejoice.
The tombs are broken at the trumpet's voice.
Life finds its Resurrection and rebirth,
Out of the living mystic womb of earth.

XXI.

The World with its four elements we see;
Within, a naked Goddess dances free.
The water and the wind, the earth and fire,
And That which doth beyond them all aspire.

A MEDITATION

Spear and Cauldron, Sword and Stone,
Holy Tetragrammaton!

Wake, O Gods, the sleeping mind
To your voices in the wind
Echoing an ancient rhyme
Down the labyrinths of time.
Here I, naked and alone,
Kneel before the sacred stone.
Here I bow to beg your truth
Blazoned with the hallowed word.
Nerve this hand to grasp the sword
Elfin-forged with holy blade
'Gainst the demons of the shade,
And the magic sigil draw,
Sign of sanctity and awe,
Bid me in the cauldron gaze
Where the stilléd water's face,
Deep and dark as dead of night,
Spectral-rayed with mystic light,
Shows the shadows of all things,
Crowns of half-forgotten kings
And those in far off dawns unknown
That shall rise when we are gone;
Show them as a measure trod
To the piping of a God,
Whose melodies my soul entrance
Into the ecstatic dance;
Till that mighty one shall dart

In the cavern of my heart,
Consummation of desire
Like a wondrous spear of fire.

Spear and Cauldron, Sword and Stone,
Holy Tetragammaton.

THE ROAD

Pagan, pagan, what are you seeking,
Through all the days of your long earthly tread?
Your sunrise and moonrise what chances are bringing?
And where will your travelling footsteps be led?

Pagan, pagan, sad is your heart now;
Stranger you are in a world not your own.
Its clamorous voices are echoing round you.
Though in the crowd, you still travel alone.

When the fires of sunset in heaven are burning,
When over the hills blows the wind of the dawn,
Then voices ancestral within you are calling.
Still knows the wildwood the dance of the faun.

Pagan, pagan, what are you finding?
Yours is the road that winds lonely and far.
Strange are the shadows that round you come creeping.
Still through the clouds is the glint of a Star.

- WINTER -

THE NIGHT RUNE

When shadows darken,
And starlight gleams,
The ways of the Old Gods
We tread in our dreams.

Beyond good and evil
They call from afar,
In the scent of the twilight,
And in the evening star.

Let far become near,
And past become here,
And the will and the way
Of the Old Ones appear!

Through gateways of darkness
We follow the light,
O'er the rivers of dream
And the pathways of night.

So witches may fly,
Though none may them see.
When body lies sleeping,
Soul wandereth free.

Let far become near,
And past become here,
And the will and the way
Of the Old Ones appear!

ELEGY FOR A DEAD WITCH

To think that you are gone,
Over the crest of the hills
As the Moon passed from her fullness,
Riding the sky,
And the White Mare
Took you with her.
To think that we will wait
Another life
To drink wine from the horns,
And leap the fire.
Farewell from this world,
But not from the Circle.
That place that is
Between the worlds
Shall hold return in due time.
Nothing is lost.
The half of a fruit
From the tree of Avalon
Shall be our reminder,
Among the fallen leaves
This life treads underfoot.
Let the rain weep.
Waken in the sunlight
From the Realms of Sleep.

HALLOWEEN

Halloween, the witches' night,
When the stars are shining bright,
Scattered through the frosty sky,
And the wind is blowing high.
Hear the whispers through the dark,
By the branches bare and stark,
As the fallen leaves below
Dance and rustle to and fro.
Sound that almost is a voice
Softly calls us to rejoice,
And in answer to the call
Of the pagan festival,
Somewhere in the mind's dark deep
Memory wakes from its sleep.
Long ago the dance we trod,
Honouring the Eldest God.
Long ago the wine was poured
To a horned and heathen lord.
Round about the bonfire's blaze
Danced we so in elder days,
While the dark hills echoing
Answered to our carolling.
Now the magic night is still
On the forest and the hill,
In a later lifetime pent,
Have we yet no merriment?
Or by the flickering candles' light
Shall we meet on Witches' night?
Care we not who says us nay,

We will go our ancient way.
Care we not for scorn or wrath,
We will tread our pagan path.
Gliding through a midnight wood,
Muffled close in cloak and hood,
Or where candles light the gloom,
Meeting in some hidden room,
Where the circle we may trace,
Making it a magic place,
With the fume of incense smoke
Shall our craft the Powers invoke
Of the Old Art Magical
Hidden deep within us all.
When between two worlds we stand,
Life and death are hand in hand.
Past and present joined may be
In our vision's fantasy,
And the door may swing ajar
On the future stretched afar,
Or our souls reached out to know
Wise ones of the long ago.
Hand to hand and heart to heart,
Merry meet and merry part.
Many strange things shall be seen
Ere the dawn, on Halloween.

QUATRAIN TO SUBTOPIA

No weed will grow upon their concrete floor.
With greed they're starved, with gracious living pale,
And hanging on each pastel-painted door,
There reads a little notice: "Souls for Sale".

MOON AND SEA

Black horses of night
From the edge of the sky
Shake their starry bridles.
Moonrise is nigh.

This is the white Moon
That shone on Babylon,
Before the pagan years
Were past and gone.

The doves of Ishtar
Crooned to her of love.
The incense of Egypt
Rose cloudily above.

The years' slow caravan
Passes ceaselessly.
For what strange things have been,
Stranger yet may be.

Naught is there new,
Save what has been forgotten;
And an antique soul
May wait the unbegotten.

White goddess Moon,
Pearl of mystery,
Whom the worshipping tide
Follows from the sea.

The waters of the soul
Have currents and tides,
And an unknown sky
Where a white Moon rides.

The chalk-white rocks
Of this forsaken shore
Yield star-flower fossils
Of aeons before.

So those other waters,
On the shores of the mind,
Yield Moon, stars and flowers,
After their kind.

THE SUSSEX WITCH

She passes through the village street,
As evening shadows fall.
The full moon climbs the winter sky,
The trees are bare and tall.

What is the secret that they share,
Shadow and moon and tree,
And little laughing breeze that makes
The dead leaves dance with glee?

They know their kin. The owl cries
His greeting out to her.
Now the last house and garden's past,
The Down's ridge rises bare.

A climbing moonlit path she sees,
That was a trodden road
Ere conquering Rome or Norman proud
O'er Downland ever strode.

It leads to where, beneath the turf,
The outlines she can trace
Of barrow and of sacred ring,
That may mark the Old Gods' place.

The moon rides high. The years roll back,
Are with her garments shed.
Naked she dances out the ring
First wrought by hands long dead.

The blood leaps wild within her veins,
As swifter spins the dance,
Her wide eyes fixed upon the moon,
Her senses rapt in trance.

And though no feet of flesh and blood
Walked with her to that ground,
She knows she does not dance alone
That magic circle's round.

THE KINDRED

They hear the wind in the trees,
And even in the lamp-lit street
Faster their pulses beat,
Because of the wind in the trees.

And when the pale light gleams
On the blade of an old sword,
A half-forgotten lord
Sways their blood's deep dreams.

To them the dark winds croon
A whisper that's almost a name,
For once an arrow came
From the bow of the wanton moon.

With sweetly venomed dart
To pierce each pious garb,
Till its enchanted barb
Sank in the hidden heart.

THE PLANETARY POWERS

Saturn, orb of Time's black night,
Strangely ringed with glowing light,
In the dark and silent mine
Gleam thy jewels crystalline.

Jupiter, the azure sky
Echoes to the thunder's cry,
When the summer rain doth yield
Peace and plenty to the field.

Armoured Mars with shining sword
Bravely treads, the warrior lord,
Roded in red; his weapon fierce
Raised the mystic gate to pierce.

Sovereign Sun of splendid gold,
Let thy robe of light unfold.
Field and forest, flower and lawn,
Wait thee at the gates of dawn.

Touch of Venus' hand shall start
Love and wonder in the heart,
When her naked limbs are seen
'midst each summer's verdant green.

Ever young, bright Mercury,
Winging swift o'er land and sea;
News of joy and secrets rare
Brings the Gods' gay messenger.

Three-fold Luna's silver light
Spreads enchantment o'er the night,
Swaying by her witchery
Tides of air and earth and sea.

Mystic powers, in number seven,
Show their symbols thus in heaven,
And on us their influence shine,
Bodied so in forms divine.

ON THE NIGHT OF THE FULL MOON

On the night of full moon fly
Hosts of vampire – succubae.
Everywhere the moon may shine,
There they seek their magick wine.
Over forest, over town,
In pointed hat and tattered gown.
Over wasteland, over roof,
Leaving print of cloven hoof.
Taking any shape they care,
Bat or owl, cat or hare.
Over hedge and over stream,
(indecipherable) into the land of dream.
There your darkest wish fulfil,
There by magick work your will.
Secret truth is in this rhyme,
Secrets hid from ancient time.

10th July 1977

THE PAGAN CAROL

The holly and the ivy
When they are both full grown,
Of all the trees that are in the wood,
The holly bears the crown.

Oh, the rising of the sun
And the running of the deer,
The playing of the merry organ,
Sweet singing in the choir,

The holly bears a blossom
As white as lily flower,
And when the Sun is newly born,
'Tis at the darkest hour

The holly bears a berry
And blood-red is its hue,
And when the Sun is newly born,
It maketh all things new.

The holly bears a leaf
That is for ever green,
And when the Sun is newly born,
Let love and joy be seen.

The holly and the ivy
The mistletoe entwine,
And when the Sun is newly born,
Be joy to thee and thine.

A Hymn to Hermes

Helmeted Hermes, Leader of the Dead,
Shepherd of souls who pace the realms of dread,
Light me the path into thy hollow hill
When I the dark and mystic way fulfil.
Thy curious wand, enwrÈathed every way
With guardian snakes that vivify and slay,
Be unto me a sign of ended strife,
Opposites balanced on the Tree of Life.
Herald divine, the Eight-spoked Wheel that spins,
Round of our joys, our sorrows, and our sins,
Bright laughter's lord, incline to our dim earth,
And all our ways enlighten with thy mirth,
Born of the Gods and that immortal Light
That, conquering chaos, demons puts to flight.
Thrice master of all noble alchemy,
Strike us with sigilled wand that we may see
Spells in thy symbols, eloquent and mute,
That shall the formless and the dark transmute
With mystic Stone that turneth all to gold,
When we thy Splendour's vision may behold.

POEM ON THE DEATH OF A WITCH

We are not sad, Virgilio,
To know you've passed the gate,
Through which one day we all must go,
When summoned by our fate.

You've found the kingdom that we seek,
The faery realm serene.
Before us is the winter bleak,
For you, the summer's green.

You've passed in honour and in love
From those who knew you well.
The memory you've left shall prove
An ever-potent spell.

The foe that to you did his worst
Still could not make you hate,
And by his own mean self accursed,
Sees you inviolate.

Old friend, we will remember you
When Halloween draws nigh,
And when the moon comes shining through
The clouded midnight sky.

We'll know your laugh upon the wind,
You'll dance with us the ring,
E'en though our mortal eyes be blind
To all but earthly thing.

We are the bound, and you the free,
    Yours is the Gods' own land;
    But somewhere in eternity,
    Again we'll clasp your hand.

1970

THE WATER CITY

Sunk beneath the blue Atlantic,
There the Water City lies,
That was once the place of wisdom,
ëNeath the stars of elder skies.

Silence wraps its shrouded temples,
And the fish swim to and fro,
Where amid the stones gigantic,
Wizard priests were wont to go.

Far beneath the waves of ocean,
There its cities lie asleep,
Haunted by the silent gliding
Shapes of monsters of the deep.

And a mystic song arises
From the dark cyclopean stone,
With the tide, as men lie dreaming,
Having nought of earthly tone;

Singing of an elder Eden,
When the Goddess Earth was young;
Echoing the first primeval
Love-song that was ever sung.

Shining stands the Water City,
Like a pearl we see it gleam,
Through the twilight and the moonlight,
In the country of our dream;

Outside Time, for She is timeless,
She, the Queen of all therein,
Goddess-Mother of all living,
Veiled with shadows and with sin.

So Her face is dark with terror,
For the Veil alone we see,
Till the Water City rises,
And we find our liberty.

THE HAUNTED LAKE

The haunted lake turns up its eye
Unto the white and leprous moon.
A cold air whispers through the sky
That She is coming soon.

A twisted thorn with pointing hand
The path to that wan water shows,
And in fantastic saraband
A dancing elf-light glows.

The midnight wood is dark and deep,
And underneath the branches bare
The printless footprints rush and creep
To greet Her presence there,

A herald owl cries before,
As in Her garments glistening white
She walks upon that faery shore,
The Goddess-Queen of Night.

The mortal man that doth Her see
Shall go enchanted all his days.
No fairer love shall for him be,
Nor equal to Her praise.

CANDLEMAS

Sun and fire warm the earth
At Old Candlemas returning.
Through the long night see it shine,
Magic in the thin flames burning.

In the clouded vault of heaven,
Jewelled stars that sparkle clear,
Dance in their eternal measure
Through the changes of the year.

Snowdrops through the frozen mould
Force a greanleaf blade again,
While above the brances bare
Shake in freezing wind and rain.

Crouched upon the cottage floor,
See the witch that eyes the flames,
Whispering as the candles burn,
Naming age-old pagan names.

Primal powers of Death and Life,
Called on by her invocation,
Viewless presences draw near,
As she weaves the incantation.

Knotting in the witches' cord
The immortal spells that bind,
Through the winter and the dark,
Love to Life and Hope to Mind.

TO THE NECRONOMICON

Thou mystic volume of forbidden lore,
Writ by Alhazred's trembling hand of yore,
Where dost thou hide? What nameless guardian
Witholds thy pages from the eyes of man?
In some black lightless crypt art thou inhumed
That is by nought but spiders' eyes illumed?
What mummied hand doth hold thee in its grasp,
Where dust of ages films thy jewelled clasp?
Or art thou locked in secret sanctuary
Where none but the initiate may see,
Where silent robéd priests the scrolls unfold
From cavern chests of ebony and gold
In Schamballah, deep in Agharti's fane,
Which snow-clad summits guard from the profane
So that our learning, fragmented and brief,
Hears but the whispered name of Al Azif?
The Lords of Silence – deemed they better so,
That this the outer world should little know
Of all thy secrets, monstrous and malign,
Or the dark splendours that thou dost enshrine
And yet, across the regions desolate,
The wandering winds may wail about thy gate,
With fleshless fingers plucking at the door
To hidden places sealed an age before,
Shunned with stark fear by travellers that wend
Those lonely ways, and long for journey's end,
Crowding about the camp-fire's fitful light
That shields them from the demon-haunted night.
Or mouldering in some ancient castle's hall,

Is there a shelf that none doth now recall,
Upon it an old book, close-locked and grim,
Lit by a gleam through windows rich and dim,
Bound with an eldritch magic seal unknown,
That some strange wizard ancestor did own?
Fearful and yet desired; O magic tome,
In some dark catacomb, what grinning gnome
Crouches by thee? And by the light of day
Would thine abhorréd letters melt away,
Crumbling to dust? No, thou too dost partake
Of that fell verse the Arab sage did make:
That is not dead which can eternal lie;
And with strange aeons, even death may die.

FAREWELL

Deaprting, you leave me,
Stretch out the thread that links us together
Far and thin as the skein
Of the veins that bind the wandering blood;
Seeing no vision
Save through the bottom of the glass of sorrow,
Or a mirror warped in the heat of pain.
So I make you a pattern of incantation
To turn you away from the lying cold glass,
Call you out of the crowding walls.
You shall bud like a branch in spring
When the thin life spurts again
In the fountains of the trees.
You shall see again the arch of the sky
Blossom with stars at the bright day's end,
And the naken new moon like a witch's knife
Circle the earth and enchant it for you.
As the years open their buds,
And spill their winged seed on the wind of life,
And crystallise their gems,
So shall love run through your life like rain through a tree.
Remember this singer then.

THE CASTLE

Before Caer Ochren
The winding of the ways is long,
Before you come to the smooth white walls
Shining like pearl in the darkness.

Before the Glass Castle
Are the spirals of the maze,
The lifting veils and the closing shadows,
And the murk of night upon all.

Before the Castle of Sorrow
Is drowning in the sea of darkness.
The last light of the Moon, with her sharp sickle,
The toothed portcullis and the quaking drawbridge.

Before Caer Arianhod
Are the Gate and the Guardian,
The armoured rider with a naked sword.
Cold is the air as he passes by.

Red and flaming is the fire
Within the hall of that high queen.
Filled with bright wine is the bowl in her hand.
Her eyes are blue and shining as the sea.
How many shall go therein and return?

Her vesture half of blue and half of red,
Life and death are in her two hands.
In the deeps of her bowl, the perilous vision.
How many shall enter before her and return?

Through the empty hall, a wind of laughter
Whirls us, frail straws, back across the drawbridge.
Our boldness moved the Powers to mirth and mercy.
How many shall enter the Castle and return?

Black and silver is the wood of bare trees,
Wherein by moonlight treads her unicorn's hoof.
Bare on his bare back she rides, veiled in her own bright hair.
How many shall enter the secret realms and return?

A Toast to the Old Ones

Throughout, about,
And round about,
Or be it dark or light,
We round it here,
When moon shines clear,
At witching hour of night.

We spirits call
Unto our thrall,
All in Dame Hecate's name,
To aid our will,
For good or ill,
And speed our wild game.

A lantern's glow
Our ring doth show,
All robed in cloak and hood.
Let none be nigh,
That may us spy,
When meet we in the wood.

Be blest fourfold
With prayer so old,
That here join hand in hand.
Food and clothing,
Home and loving,
Luck be to our band.

While stars do shine,
We pledge the wine,
To Them we've worshipped long.
Mortal and ghost,
Join in the toast,
So may our Craft be strong.

They who before,
In days of yore,
Were even such as we,
Out of the past,
Shall come at last,
To wish us "Blessed Be....."

So met by stealth,
We drink a health,
Unto the Gods of Old.
Nor shall there fail,
The witch wassail,
Nor shall their fire grow cold.

In time's dark night,
It shineth bright,
For love and freedom here;
And when at last,
Death's gate be passed,
We'll enter without fear.

- THE WITCH'S CHANT -

Darksome night and shining Moon,
Hell's dark mistress Heaven's Queen
Harken to the Witches' rune,
Diana, Lilith, Melusine!

Queen of witchdom and of night,
Work my will by magic rite.
Earth and water, air and fire,
Conjured by the witch's blade,

Move ye unto my desire,
Aid ye as the charm is made!
Queen of witchdom and of night,
Work my will by magic rite.

In the earth and air and sea,
By the light of moon or sun,
As I pray, so mote it be.
Chant the spell, and be it done!

Queen of witchdom and of night,
Work my will by magic rite.

The Doreen Valiente Foundation

The Doreen Valiente Foundation is a charitable trust dedicated to the protection and preservation of material relating to Pagan practices, spirituality and religion. The Foundation is also dedicated to researching and interpreting this material and making such research and the material itself accessible to the public for the benefit of wider education and the advancement of knowledge in this unique landscape of living cultural and religious heritage.

The Foundation was established in 2011 and received legal ownership of Doreen Valiente's entire legacy of artefacts, books, writings, documents, manuscripts and copyrights under a deed of trust that permanently prevents the sale or splitting up of the collection and prohibits the making of profit through exploitation of the collection. This means that every penny earned by the Foundation, including the proceeds of the sale of this book) is spent on persuing its goals and charitable objects as above.

The Foundation runs a number of ongoing projects, working towards the establishment of a permanent museum home for the collection and the physical creation of a Centre For Pagan Studies which was the name of the organisation of which Doreen was patron shortly before her death in 1999. The Foundation succeeded in a campaign to have Doreen awarded a Heritage Blue Plaque which was unveiled at her former home in Brighton, England in 2013 and has ongoing plans to honour other important Pagan figures in a similar way - at the time of publication the campaign for Gerald Gardner's blue plaque is underway. The Foundation is also organising conferences, talks and exhibitions as well as engaging with the global community in matters of religious history and heritage.

More information about Doreen Valiente and The Doreen Valiente Foundation, including foundation membership, details of events and activities, purchase of Doreen Valiente merchandise, books etc and donations can be found at:

www.doreenvaliente.org